YOURS IN SOLITUDE & SOLACE

ISHRAT UMAR

Made with ❤ on the Notion Press Platform
www.notionpress.com

My book *YOURS IN SOLITUDE & SOLACE* is dedicated to
my loving caring Husband MOHD. UMAR

Contents

Contents

Contents

Contents

Contents

Preface

I am Ishrat Umar a part-time author. A few years ago, I put my first step in the literary world and wrote 7 books,.one in Hindi and rest in English. Writing is my passion. inherited by my parents'. I am polite, positive, honest, hard- working and loving person. For me, humanity is the best religion. My parents molded us towards academics and sports. My mantra in life is bloom where you are planted and believe that poetry is soothing and it connects the world. Imagination revolves around me. My own family helped me to fly, I am grateful to all of them. Now I am following my dreams. I accept life with all its challenges. God is my pillar of strength from other world but my loving, caring husband (a retired para- military officer) and my family remained my strength to be.

In the realms of creativity, there exists a boundless space where the imagination takes flight, defying the constraints of reality and ushering us into a world of endless possibilities. It is within this vast expanse that the collection of poems titled YOURS IN SOLITUDE & SOLACE finds its dwelling.

This anthology is an exploration of the human imagination, capturing the ethereal essence that resides within each of us. It is celebration of the profound power of imaginations, which serves as a bridge connecting the tangible and intangible, the known and unknown. Through the rhythmic credence of words, the poet ventures into unchartered territories, inviting readers to embark on a journey that transcends time and space.

Within pages of my poetry book, you will encounter poetic musings and traverse the realm of fantasy, love, day today happenings, fast changes of times and introspection. Each poem a portal to a world of vivid imagery and evocative emotions, beckons you to leave the mundane behind and delve into the tapestries of extraordinary.

The poems of my book are invitation to embrace the magic within and unlock the doors of perception. They are reminder that the human spirit thrives on the wings of creativity, forever yearning to break free from the constraints of everyday life. Within every- verse the poet invites you to join in the surreal, where dreams became tangible and words become whispers from the cosmos. I feel poetry is heavenly bliss, which imparts pleasure and contentment to both the poets and readers as well. The strength of my poems is their simplicity and elegant style.it is this simplicity which makes a deep impact on readers.

WE

We have right tunings
But feel something missing.
We ponder and ponder
But return- back to square one.
The worst question with no answer is, hey!
What people will say?
Please, please be yourself
Do not worry much about other's say?
We are never afraid
Negativity make us shaky
Off and on it forbade.
Why we degrade?
We are our destiny's masters
We are muqadder ka Sikander.
Why hesitate
It is a question of our fate.

FOREST RANGER

Forest rangers are the eyes and ears of the forest.
They are protecting the wildlife and landscape of the forest.
They are nature's lovers.
They move in open gypsy with big hats.
Life of a forest ranger at sunset
Red is the arch of the night mare sky.
Red are the mountains beneath,
Bright where, hundreds of black birds leap high.
Forest rangers enjoy their surroundings.
Their government job is satisfactorily with enough funding.
Their cottages are in dense forest,
Surrounded by barbed fencing.
Chirping of birds, make morning and evening very pleasing.
The forest rangers are bold and dutiful.
For animals their acts are blissful.

THE OCEAN

The ocean is beautiful as well as vast.
It teaches us to move fast.
The life of marine animals is secured by it.
Their life activities are secured by it.
Ocean teaches us to be adventurous,
Face uncertainty and be courageous.
The cold water sweeps the feet,
As if waves of ocean whisper.
Calling us to soft, moist sand.
The ocean takes care of each wave,
Till it gets to shore.
A raindrop spends a lifetime
Falling alone, and it meets the ocean
With gratitude.
The ocean has its stores
It has its tides.
In its depth, it has pearls too.
The sight of ocean is gracious and amazing too.

THE DAY YOU WENT AWAY

The day we sent our son to Sherwood,
After his departure, our home was, salient wood.
He was our Robin hood.
As if every nook and corner was calling Robinhood.
The 12 years old, smart lad settled in middle school.
There he was happy and cheerful.
Sending him to hostel, was our decision,
With his co-operation.
His younger sister was crying
We were counseling.
Life is full of turfs and furrows.
It looked, as if life is full of sorrows.
Time flies fast
Years after years past.
He completed his high school with flying colors.
Now we are waiting for his arrival.
Still, we are remembering the day, he went away

A LONELY BOAT ON VAST SEA

Carry on with pace
Harmony and smiles.
It is beautiful nature
Enhanced by the presence of the lonely boat,
As if it is a creature.
The boat is carrying the passengers.
The vast surface of water,
Is gleamed by the rising sun nearer.
The movement of boat depends on ripples of water weaves
Still the boatman sings.
The passengers are enjoying the cool breeze,
Sitting with ease.
The bright sun rise is scattering golden rays
Which are absorbed by waves.
How fast the boat moves
The boatman has clues.
It is his routine,
To carry passengers from one bank to another.

STARRY NIGHT

As a man wish with all his might
He realizes, his vision on stars' twinkling bright.
He watches the starry night,
With much passion and love.
Stars are glowing on clean, blue sky.
Many constellations
Such a beautiful sight
Which neither be assumed nor be made on
Artificial sights.
It is natural, cool brightness of stars,
Though millions of miles away.
Their light preamble through layers of atmosphere,
Is the reason behind their shinning and twinkling.
After all a starry night is gift of amazing nature,
Which we absorb and feel elated
And try to nurture.

NEW YEAR NEW BEGINNINGS

Boarding of flight 2024 has been announced.
Your luggage should only contain,
The best souvenirs from 2023, you found.
The bad and sad moments should be left in the garage.
The duration of flight should be twelve months,
With limited luggage.
The next stop overs will be health, love and joy
Well-being, peace and harmony.
*The captain offers you the following menu_*
A cocktail of friendship,
A supreme of health
A grain of prosperity
A bowl of excellent news
A salad of success
A cake of happiness
Accompanied by burst of laughter.
New year new beginning.
You and your family be blessed.

HAPPINESS IS A CHOICE

Happiness shows positive outcome of different ways.
It depicts mental well-being and over all longevity always.
Happy people are more successful
Not rich or poor, but always hopeful.
Happiness is fine feeling,
Which propels us towards satisfaction and well-being.
Positive emotions do good to our brains,
Not compelling us towards loses and gains.
The inner quest for happiness brings
Composites of life's satisfaction.
Happiness is a state of mind.
Feeling that everything is fine.
Though ups and downs of life ,
Are always challenging
But happiness is a choice
It is our perspectives--- how to enjoy?

DESIRES

Desires are countless
Why be restless?
Balancing is precious
Why always be curious?
Many desires are useless
But comparison pushes.
Endless efforts
Restless souls
Frequent success.
Positive thoughts
Control desires.
Luck plays
Unexpected favors.
Why haste
Be passionate.
Slow and steady wins the race?
Desires, desires and desires.

TIME-TRAVEL

Saw the time and lights when we were young
Gaze with eyes, full of wonders
To a time, when we were innocents
To contents to live in the moments.
Time travels is imaginary
Impossible people say.
Not even a scientist extraordinary.
Can see things that fade aways.
The time lost
Can never be regained.
Memories lost
Our search is again
In vain.
The beginning is determined by the end.
It only really starts when we all stop.
Time is precious.
How its travels we handle and remain conscious.

A LANTERN HANGING ON A LEAFLESS TREE

Rest is to refresh my mind set.
It is beautiful sunset
Far away the sun is at rest
I was returning from my evening walk.
A silent lantern
Hanging on a quite leafless tree
Sending message of loneliness
For me it is happiness.
I love walking alone
My shadow is my companion.
Being a nature lover, I enjoy solitudes'
Have positive attitudes.
Merging colors of sky
Spattering lots of joy.

ALL I WANT FOR CHRISTMAS IS YOU

You are my soulmate.
For me, only you are great.
From last one year you are struggling
For your well-being.
Each day you are in my prayers.
God knows our helplessness'.
But all I want for Christmas is you.
I will be lifeless without you.
Our fine tuning,
Were ideals, for cousins and siblings.
Your etiquette and nice smile,
Was amazing.
Today, your blank face is questioning
Something,
Only I can imagine.
My heart beat and soul are for you.
All I want for Christmas is you.

NEW JOURNEY

After passing through three stages of life successfully
The last stage i.e. old age is a new journey.
We accept it gracefully.
Our wrinkles hide many stories.
Which leave behind many quaries.
It is relaxing time for us,
But texting time for nears and dears.
Our new journey has ample time
Though health challenges are there.
We are passing this new journey happily.
All responsibilities are done faithfully.
No worries for future,
No attention seeking,
No unfulfilled dreams,
No much carving for food.
We are happily accepting challenging times.
The new journey of old age is fine.

FOR PEOPLE WHO PASSED 70 & MOVING TOWARDS 80

After loving my, parents, siblings, spouse, children, grand-children,
I have now started loving myself?
I have realized that I am not atlas,
The world does not have require anymore!
I have stopped bargaining from vendors.
I have stopped telling the elderly
They have already told the story
Now I learnt not to correct people.
Even when I know they are wrong.
Peace is more important than perfection.
I have learnt not to bother about crease of my shirt,
For me, personality speaks louder than appearance.
I walk away from people who don't value me.
I have learnt not to be embraced by my emotions.
It is my emotions that make me human.
I am doing what makes me happy,
I am responsible for my happiness.

ON THIS VALENTINE'S DAY

Every year valentine day reminds
Love and affection rewinds,
Beautiful gifts, red roses are exchanged
As if love is blooming again
With freshness
Full of sweet memories and happiness.
Our minds elated
With lots of sweet- sour experiences.
After passing 48 years of togetherness,
Hopes are diminishing on this valentine day.
I will be under the magic of my prayers,
For his recovery and well- being.
Now he is better but not remembering
Enthusiasm vanishes.
No celebrations
Only sweet memories.
Time changes and life goes on
Happy valentine day to all

BEAUTIFUL HANDS

Beautiful hands
One thanks
New manicure techniques
Which make hands unique.
Nice simple rings
On soft fingers
Painted nails
Shows our love and care.
We want to love ourselves for
ever.
Time spared
On our own world
Is positive affair.
Love yourself
Love your body.
Always be ready to look nice and classy.
My face is like moonlight
Why not my personality be bright?

I & YOU

I and you together
Become we, as we remember.
So much time we spent together
So much amusement.
Fights full of entertainment
Bring us closer
Solves our purpose.
Pretty good space.
We impart each other.
Without any haste
Life's lessons made us companions.
Now we are responsible.
I and you are lovable couple.
Full of wit and humor,
And tussles with ifs and buts.
You are my sunshine.
Will always be, by your side
Is, where I want to be.

BLOOM

Bloom where you are planted.
I have bloomed and flowered
A thousand times in this life.
Soft and sweet language.
Whispers like dreams,
A flower may bloom,
Or it may wither
But I deserve love.
Do not sentence us to your grandeur
Where no foliage remains
Where the soil is rocky
The base is stone.
That does not drain.
I bloom without any rain.
I am happy with everything.
Sometimes I feel like a flower
Who blooms with light showers.

BETRAYAL

Betrayal shatters the foundation of trust.
People, have- to trust.
Someone like close friends,
relatives or neighbors.
When emotions harbor
But what to do with double standards?
Socializing is diminishing
Self- centered attitude is flourishing.
Where are lovely, trustworthy friends and nice neighbors?
Why people are betrayed?
Betrayal leaves us feeling hurt,
Angry and disillusioned
One gets shattered,
Physically, emotionally and mentally,
If one's near and dear betrayals.

MYSTERY

Life is a mystery,
It flourishes, hurts, and becomes history.
Mystery of life is solved now and then.
The tangled mystery remains mystery.
Years after years.
New problems are raised,
But solutions of them are beyond our understandings.
Hold fast to dreams.
For if dreams die,
Life will be like a broken winged bird
That can, not fly.
Hold fast to dreams.
For, when dreams vanish
Life is a lovely field
Submerged in colors of mystery
How to solve and go?

IN MY DREAMS

I think big and dream big.
I dream of sound health of my husband,
Who always remained a pillar of strength
I dream of cure of every ailment.
Why there is so much pain and misery?
I dream of peace and harmony.
I dream of the world full of happiness,
Excitement and perseverance.
I dream of the people,
Socializing and mingling with each other.
No differences of caste and creed,
Some glimpses of yester years'
May God fulfill our sweet dreams,
Which are far away from reality,
But our thoughts are bound to happen occasionally.

DRENCHED

We were in a well- lit market place
Suddenly it was raining
We were under an umbrella, feeling safe.
There was hustle bustle.
But businesses were as usual.
Brisk selling, shop-keepers were casual.
As it was festive season (Rakshabandhan)
Ladies were finishing their shopping.
But, don't want to halt without any reason.
So many colorful umbrellas
As it was raining with cats and dogs.
With wet shoes everyone was running to their cars.
Packed parking and heavy showers
Too much honking.
Everyone, has, to wait and watch.
It was an amazing experience
Of shopping on a rainy day.

DRIZZLING MORNINGS

In a drizzling morning
Watching through a window pane,
Someone becomes insane
There is someone's (disease) increasing pain.
Drizzling rain
Incites someone for game
An artist tries to paint
Natural beauty on paper again and again.
Drizzling rain
Evokes children to play in rain
Enjoy water and cool breeze with rain.
Teenagers are busy in mud riots.
People enjoy drizzling rain.
Through windows of fast- moving trains,
We enjoyed drizzling and heavy rains.
In our childhood,
On our roof tops too,
we were giggling and pushing each other in rain.

LIFE'S LESSONS

Life gives lessons to be light hearted.
Sometimes forget and laugh
Sometimes be tense but not enough.
Though there are many ups and downs,
But life teaches us to leave some decisions for times.
I do not know, whether I again meet some close friends
Or my nice company will slip with time.
Life reminds us that time is precious,
But some of our approaches are hilarious.
Life imparts lessens, not to fight with yourself.
But a continuous fight is going on within ourself.
Life is harsh but we love it.
Life is tough but we lead it.
Life's many lessons are on humanitarian ground
But our materialistic approach does not,
Keep things fit and fine.
Life is a wonderful experience and enjoy it.

MONSOON

It is raining heavily
We came out casually
Without umbrella,
Under a plastic sheet,
Feeling safe and fine
We are safe together.
Across the sky
Lightning dancing
Herky- jerky
It burns with a headless joy.
Behind a clapping curtain of rain
We are enjoying together, in our own frame.
Feet, completely soaked, shoes drenched.
Splashes of rain on our faces
Soothing experience
Of wonderful rain together.
We all love the rain
The way it gracefully falls on leaves.
Ground is soaking up the rain
Until it fades away.
The rain washes away
Sorrows and pains
And imparts the belief of innocence again.

MY HEART SEARCHES

A poem is caught in my mind.
Its lines stuck on my lips
Words refuse to sit on paper,
they are like butterflies.
My heart searches that poem.
A printer of his own breath.
Unravels each and wrap up around his body.
As the silk worm is chocked by his own threads
My heart searches that state of mind.
Like broken necklace of pearls
My days and nights lay scattered,
But how you kept me strung together
My heart searches that technique somewhere.
Some more suns scattered across the universe.
I am unraveling the matted locks of the sky.
Come, let us all wear mirrors
Everyone will appear attractive to the other.
My heart searches that mystery everywhere.

SISTER

My dear and precious sister,
You are more than words can say
They say good looks are only skin deep
But you are always full of love.
And that will I always keep.
I am proud of you for so many things
It is a joy when we were together
You were like cool breeze and fine weather.
You always been a calm and quite friend.
We kept our secrets with each other
In happy times and rough weather.
You always remain my pillar of strength.
At every stage of life our bonding, strengthen,
Now I cherish
the precious moments we spent together,
Fine memories and golden moments of happiness'.

YOUR SMILE

Your smile is infectious
Sometimes you are very conscious.
A smile speaks a lot,
You are aware of the reason.
Your sweet smile crushes the root.
Your smile brings sunshine to my life
And beauty into my world.
In your smile there is togetherness,
Strength and comfort.
Your smile makes you beautiful,
Far more than any make-up.
Your smile makes you happy
Be generous with your smile,
Let it light up the world around you.
Your smile light up your heart.

MYSTERY

God moves in mysterious way
Has wonders to perform
He plans his footsteps in the sea
And rides upon the storm.
Deep in unfathomable mines
Of never, failing skills.
Treasures up his bright designs
And works his sovereign will.
All is mystery beyond our wisdom.
Judge not the Lord by feeble sense
But trust him for his grace
Behind a frowning providence
He hides a smiling face.
His mysteries are endless beyond our faiths.
His purpose is risen fast
Unfolding every hour.
It may be formation of grains, fruits, vegetables,
Beautiful flowers and arrival of new-born to every life.
Mystery, mystery, mystery?

VOYAGE

When we board a plane, the chairs are adjustable,
Easy sitting with safety belts.
We fly over the world, see our country enrolled.
Like a map, save—if you desire to ---time.
Look back at the sunset, you are flying from.
If you prefer luxury liner (journey on ship)
Café' terrace, gymnasia, restaurants,
Forty- two thousand tons, route on the sea.
Speed of 0.24 knots, warm days, cool nights
Far from the salvos and the sunken mines
The bulb blow- up under the water line.
Lutes were ringing, youths were singing.
Dwelled my heart with feeling strange
Bluer grew the heavens above us
Wider grew the spirits rangers
One bright image struggles back.

TWO STRANGERS

In our neighborhood there were two strangers.
For years they never talked to any neighbor.
Their office hours were same.
Sometimes they were behaving like insane.
We were annoyed of their queer ways.
Their late- night parties were order of the day.
They remain busy in their own ways.
Their neighbors were fed-up of their attitude anyway.
One night a massive fire broke-out on 3rd floor
Two teenagers were in deep sleep on that floor.
Those two strangers with blankets jumped into the burning inferno,
Took the children on their back,
Came out shouting for help.
Two precious lives were saved by them,
The neighbors were ashamed of their attitude towards them.
Aloofness was their style, but actually
Those two strangers were nice human-being.
Humanity first is our religion.

YELLOW UMBRELLA

Day by day time moves unnoticed
softly like a stranger.
I want to enjoy rain with my lovely yellow umbrella.
It reminds me when I was younger.
when the wind was grinding
With its fusing melody.
I was holding my yellow umbrella tightly.
I saw it got inverted and tried to run away.
I still remembered the beauty of my wet umbrella anyway.
It embraced me warmly, like I have never been.
It is different now.
My yellow umbrella flew, like many old things did
There is a certain time,
When you can- not, be mugged, no more.
Or you simply let yourself go.

SILENCES

The silence of high vaulting sky
The dream-like beauty all around.
The silent spread of moon, is a round.
Quite are the branches of every tree.
The birds in the valley have gone salient all
And salient is the greenery, that wraps the hills.
In the lap of night,
nature itself is fallen asleep.
The silence, such a spell of magic casts;
That the very flow of Yamuna only imparts silences.
As if a procession is going on without a whisper,
Constantly on the move.
The caravan of the stars is silent
There is silence among forests, hills and rivers.
As if in contemplation deep,
there is silence of nature.
My heart is at peace and I love silences and nature.

RELATIONSHIPS

Relationships are made.
Sometimes last longer
Sometimes fade.
The relationship of parents with their children is very strong
But with the passage of time, it feeble.
It is sign of growing up.
The relationship with friends is stronger,
But due to lack of time it is like an onlooker.
The relationship between teacher and taught,
Is up to school days,
Otherwise sooner or later it fades away.
The relationship between husband and wife,
Is just a compromise.
From time to time, they are fed up with each other
But still it lasts longer.
Happily, ever after does not, simply happen,
Fine relationships are no accident.
Life is like riding a bicycle, to keep your balance,
You must keep on moving.

BROKEN DREAMS

Dreams are broken.
They bring us into unique, colorful, hazy stories
Sometimes there are broken dreams
But I collect myself and reach to my dreams.
As promises are broken,
so our dreams fade away.
Dream I once held like a shinning object,
Like a glowing star just wished upon.
A sun promising a pristine day,
Has gone away.
I am left to gasping
Illusive petals of dreams
Like petals of a rose,
Dropped on to the palm of my hand.
No longer a flower but still leaving
A fragrance to make up my loss.

MIRROR

Never trust a mirror
Because it is full of errors.
Beauty is skin deep
But the mirror brings out one from sleep.
Your reflection can not tell you
Everything you mean to me.
Never trust a mirror
For it only shows your skin.
And if you think that it dictates your worth
It is time you introspect.
The mirror reflects your life,
The mirror can- not show the best of you.
For, you are much more than you can see.
Mirror, mirrors on the wall
Tell me what is real, the past or the future!
How I wish you could create a clone like me?

BLANK PAGE

Our arrival is our parents' delight.
We start life like a blank page, filled with light.
Early stages of life pass easily with parents' love.
Our blank page is neat and clean like a dove.
The blank page of our teen-age years gets some hazy shadows,
Which are replaced by our future worries'
After success in board exams, we again cook new stories,
Which imparts colors to our life's blank pages.
After job and settlement with our life partner,
Again, a blank page, surfaces, clearer.
With the arrival of new-born,
priorities change and the blank page is full of humor.
Precious memories are erased.
Again, a blank page is filled with responsibilities.
Life on faster pace leaves behind many tragedies.
Now at sun-set of life, we want a blank page
Our mindset changes with the speed of time,
Leaving behind a blank page (on our mind).

JOURNEY OF A STEAM ENGINE

A yesteryears' locomotive
With passengers of different motives.
Running on rails,
Leaving behind footprints of times.
Leaving lots of smoke in the sky.
A cloud's silent groan, as it flies ups and down.
The shoveling of coal
The roaring of fire.
The grunts of the stoker as he works into the night.
Faster than fairies, faster than witches
Bridges and houses, hedges and ditches,
All through the meadows, green- fields and cattle.
All the sights of the hills and plane's
And here is a mill and there is a river
The green fields, dancing peacocks
Herds of sheep, goats and cows.
Each a glimpse and gone forever.

YOU & ME

You and me, make the perfect twosome
Why we are now quarrelsome?
Why we are lost with each other?
Why not we introspect each other?
Tension between us is unbearable.
Life is unpredictable
Love blooms or perishes soon.
Why not we rectify the problem soon?
Your respect for me
Has always been enduring.
I hope I return with it
With affection, which is everlasting.
Let us try to sort out the things
Not get lost with the simmering tension within.
Life is short, life is sweet,
give space and enjoy it.

SADNESS

We are all so different
And yet so much the same.
Everyone, in some way or the other
Experience the kind of pain.
Everyone has things
They wish not to recall.
Into each life,
Some rain must fall.
Hurt and pain
There is much to gain.
Peace and love
It is all the same.
Confusion and doubts
We are not without.
We weep, we cry
We plead we try.
Life is a lesson
Learn it well.

SHADOWS

A shadow is silent
In happy time and spare time
It sets in its own notions
With not a single complain.
In childhood we made pinhole cameras
In search of image formation.
Keeping two plane mirrors on right angles
Counting many images of single thing.
It was fun to see our different shadows,
In concave and convex mirrors, put together.
Laughter, laughter and laughter
Reflection of shadows on different angles,
Made one burst into laughter.
Some hazy shadows make us suspicious.
If someone's shadow follows us
It is scary, we become anxious,
Ladies and girls get annoyed, by such behavior.

SURPRISE GIFT

I always got gifts in my school days.
Sometimes in academics, sometimes in sports.
Always got surprise gifts on my birthdays.
From siblings, parents and friends.
The most surprised gift I received
From my parents is my husband.
I never thought of about my futures
The most astonishing surprise gift, as my life partner.
Is my loving, caring, doting husband,
With him I passed more than four and a half decades.
Other surprise gifts from him are my children
Who co-operated with us on our ups and downs.
Surprise gift is precious
The value of gift does not matter.
The love and affection matters.
Our medals, certificates, trophies and appreciations
are all our surprise gifts.

IN YOUR EYES

In your beautiful, big, brown eyes
I see my whole world.
The water in your eyes is like a cool lake
My soul wants to dip in that lake.
There are lots of our stories,
Hidden in your speaking eyes
Lots of secrets, lots of novelties.
Only I understand your joys and sorrows.
What tongue can- not speak,
Your eyes silently speak.
The language of love and affection,
Is transpired between us through your eyes.
Your meaningful glances,
Whisper sometimes pain, sometimes happiness.
There is some special relationship between your eyes and mine
How wonderful it is that your eyes understand mine!

IMAGINATION

Imagine that there is no swarg
Above is only a blue sky
There are no religions only humanity,
No lies, no controversy.
Whole world is one
No boundaries
Only land and sea.
No violence,
People live with peace.
Universe is one, all are equal.
Imagine the world is devoid of materialism,
Humanity is the religion for one and all.
Truth and tranquility prevail
No distinction between male and female.
Others may consider me, only a dreamer,
Why my imagination differs?
But my imagination for universe is forever
Why don't people imagine for the better?

INDIFFERNCE

The opposite of life is not death
It is indifference.
The opposite of art is not ugliness
It is indifference.
The opposite of faith is not hearse
It is indifference.
He who has his hands lost
Will not lament his fingers frozen in frost.
When living a life, why do so indifferent?
Underneath the face of hate
Lies the smirk of love
Under the uneasy feeling of indifferences'
Lies the restless nights
Looking for that love again.
Indifference and neglect
Often do too much more damage.

BEAUTY OF WILD

In a pristine land, green forests spread beauty and greenery
The trees are rising- up
to touch sunlight curiously.
Flowers blooming in multiple colors and aromas
Butterflies are happily hopping from flowers to flowers
Savoring nectar.
Clouds of gloom behold blessed rain
to refresh nature
To burst in pleasure to bestow treasure.
Mother earth is drinking bliss in elixir of rain.
Weeds over the ground started growing
among forest inhabitants.
As each and every- being is created
with specific reason
Each has its own beauty,
glory and purpose
Anger and jealousy destroy
love, beauty, peace and harmony.
Again, rain showered bliss,
fresh air blew everywhere.
River ran through the forest,
twinkling light in smiles
Pristine glory was back on mother earth
There is greatness in highs and lows,
in dark and light.

PETALS OF HOPE

May the petals of hope teach me the art of letting go.
Petals of hope are sunshine,
food and medicine for the soul
Although there is no cure [of Alzheimer]
But petals of hope collected me together
(for my husband's well-being)
Really life is a curious thing,
As if I am struggling
Knowing there is no goal
The petals of hope I hold.
Hope is like petals [like feathers]
That perches in the soul
And sings the tune without words
And never step at all.
The petals of hope, so delicate but I hold
The leering demon days
Deride, and reason plays.
Snug as a raven in a gallows-tree
It is ancient game with me.

BUTTERFLIES

April showers
Bring swarms of butterflies
Streaming across the valley
Seeking sweet nectar.
Yellow, gold and burning bright
Red, blue and pristine white.
They bring delight to our eyes.
They do long and arduous flight.
Here today and off tomorrow,
Floating on, beautiful butterflies,
To distant bowers.
Because nature does things in fine order.
Butterfly flutter and fly
They put a sparkle in our eye.
Like a butterfly emerges, and unfolds its graceful wings
A child grows and develops with mother's love and care.
I am thankful for the times, when you encouraged me to try
For God gave me my wings,
But my parents taught me how to fly.
I will spread my wings and fly.

CROSS ROAD

You are on your own
And you prepare your feet
To cross a threshold.
At the cross roads—
The priorities change
Promises are broken
Weaknesses occur
The day become quite as night.
Sometimes we get wonderful experiences.
Life suddenly becomes expansive
Somethings have, to be felt
Too much ups and downs.
Many choices unpredictable
Life becomes unstable.
Cross roads may be positive or negative.
There may be a time of opportunity
Or a time of crisis occasionally.
Life is always challenging, live it sweetly.

SOLITUDE

(The state of being alone or remote from society)

Solitude allows me to be myself
Without any influence of anyone else.
Solitude replenishes me,
It provides introspection and positive well- being.
For me, solitude is state of peacefulness.
It cultivates my overall wellness.
In the state of solitude negativity is being brushed off.
Providing me time,
results in release of mental pressures.
I got elated doing things for myself
without any interferences.
My stress level goes down on my preferences.
Solitude boosts my creativity.
I feel relaxed, devoid of negativity.
My best me-time is, when I read a lot.
I get some me-time in my schedule for my mental health.

NEW MORNING

The colors of sunrise
Seems to fade away.
The hues of the morning mist
Seem less impressive everyway.
In front of your beauty
The mirror shy away.
The new morning seems challenging.
New thoughts and ideas are welcoming.
We are full of vigor with fresh energy.
We plan whole day accordingly.
We forget the past and greet new morning,
With lots of planning.
So many chores are completed
Schedule for meetings is decided.
What we planned at new morning,
Our whole day passes hurriedly.
Next new morning brings novel thoughts swiftly.

THE DAWN (at the beach)

At dawn, the little girl is amazed by the beauty of rising sun
The hues of orange and yellow make wonderful experience.
The cool sea- breeze
Soft wet sand underneath her feet.
Fills her heart with peace.
How the horizon is getting new beginnings
The time that is tripping by
And the dawn dew is falling
Listen to the sun, as it is rising in the sky.
Listen to the waves of water
Feel the mist in the air
And the silence calling.
The beauty of horizon runs down to the sea.
The sea so complete in itself,
Rests like a raindrop
In the hands of God.

TOGETHER WITH VIOLIN

Together we play with the beautiful instrument.
We are devoted to ours' commitment.
Music is soothing and refreshing
Learning with each-other is amusing.
We play different tunes,
as our lives spread different hues.
The sound may not make us groove.
It may not make us dance or move.
But it will surely have an impression on our soul.
The sound of violin has an important role.
Those times, when violins were made
To meet demands for sweeter sounds.
That life could offer at first sight,
Hopes for the world to come.
A distant sound from me time
Imagined but to us as real.
As the words you used to tell
What sounding board is for: it is a soul.

KANGANS

Lady's, precious hand ornaments are Kangans.
Our shringaar is incomplete without kangans.
Lady's' put on variety of kangans
Girls keep as their parents' and in-laws' Dharohars- as kangans'.
On auspicious occasions,
grand parents' gift small kangans to their grand- daughter.
Nowadays both real and artificial kangans are popular.
The twinkling sounds of kangans and payals,
Alarms someone's presence
with love and affection.
The hands decorated with hena and kangans,
Leave message of love, beauty and satisfaction.
Due to high cost of precious metal,
Families prefer to go on far off destinations.
(Instead of purchasing gold kangans.)

OUR CHILDHOOD HOME

I walked on this earth for seven decades.
I lead my childhood in a palatial, sprawling home,
Which was surrounded by a big garden.
The plants were watered by the well.
A variety of flowers on the front lawn, were accessible to all.
The kitchen garden at the backyard,
was full of green vegetables, often distributed to maids and servants.
Myself and siblings were playing badminton in our courtyard's.
In summer, we were sleeping on rooftop on wooden cots.
The sky was full of moon and stars.
We never felt lonely, or scared to dark.
Our pets were dog, cat, hens, roosters and a lamb.
Our study room has many bookshelves.
Books were our best friends.
There was no T.V. only gramophone and a radio set.
Pressing handpump, for water was our good time pass.
Two maids and three servants were working round the clock.
The rooster's crow to greet the morning was fast.
We celebrated and decorated our home on every festival,
welcomed neighbors
Socialized a lot no restrictions.
Our home sweet home was full of life
and co-ordinations.

LAST LEAF BEFORE WINTER

Nature will not be leaving you,
To languish on a branch.
Since all your mates are falling
Go join their dance.
So soon you may follow
If nature has its way.
And from the forests' trees
Now lie withered and die.
What autumn's leaf could dwell
In the dense forest alone?
Lonely leaf the last leaf
Simply wants to take rest.
To the leaves that leave,
When they fall apart, and winter is all.
Solitude is the vital final friend
As the last leaf finally descends.

WHEN TWO HEARTS MEET

When two hearts meet
There is whisper of sweet beeps,
Which they receive
Though quite strange but queer.
The sweetness continues
Until both are free to assume
Life is a bed of roses
Though roses have thorns too.
Life is sweet and moments are precious.
Two hearts believe and feel the meeting auspicious.
Their thoughts move in same directions.
Nowadays, two hearts meeting, has more precautions.
The maturity of minds,
do not allow the flow of emotions
In careless and zigzag options.
When two hearts meet, they realize as if,
they are made for each other.
There are ripples, now and then.
But the pious love overcome them.

FAIRY TALE

We remember our precious moments
How fast they vanish in minutes
Leaving behind fairy tales
We cherish them again and again.
Sometimes dreams come true
Unexpected tours and voyages.
The time passed with grand parents
The childhood memories.
Mischievous college days
All are like fairy tales.
Those times were full of joy and laughter
We never knew how they flew.
All is happily ever after.
Do the fairy artists
Paint the rainbow on the sky?
How their magic brushes
Dipped in fairy dye?

INNER PEACE

Peace of mind is soothing and comfortable
Bur inner peace is disturbing and uncomfortable.
We search ourselves many times
About our relationships with people around us.
That is, why we are forgetful,
We lose confidence but pose very dutiful.
We love ourselves but search for inner peace, goes on.
After doing lots of tasks, tired and exhausted,
We search our dreamland.
Another day starts with lots of challenges.
With inner peace of mind,
we perform without any regrets.
Our positive attitude is must for inner peace.
We are our motivation,
why disturb our inner peace?
The co-ordination of our mind and heart, is must
Why we lose our trust?
Why search for short-cuts?
We achieve inner peace,
by our honesty, truthful-ness and hard work.

MY MOTHER

For everything I am today,
Because my mother's love showed me the way.
My mother's strength and love guided me,
As if, she gave me wings to fly.
Mother, when I was young, you helped me grow (up)
And taught me all, I had to know.
Of love and trust, faith and hope.
And everything it takes to cope.
Mother, you may have thought I did not hear,
Or may be that you were not quite clear.
But all that you taught to me,
Were headed very carefully.
I will love my mother for ever
And for ever you will be
The most wonderful and lovely mother.
You mean everything to me.

YOUR LETTER

Dear father you send the message through your letter
To write more about those years,
Of changing times, achievements, promotion and love.
Continue- on writing, even after passing sixties, seventies or nineties.
Your letters are very inspiring.
Joy of writing, putting words in form of poems or stories
Is absolutely- satisfactory.
Own writings are fresh and full of intensity.
Dear father your letters are precious
Human brains are more active in later years of life,
Why to get retired from life?
We have acquired maturity.
But never want to crush our creativity.
We grew up in a troublesome world
But always tried to make it a better place to live.
Dear father, I always followed your advice,
Be happy and bloom where you are planted.

PERSEVERANCE

Perseverance pays
But it requires a lot of pertinence.
We should persevere
when it comes of our goals and dreams.
We should not give up
No matter how hard it seems.
Can-not, is the father of feeble endeavor
the root of terror and half- hearted work.
It weakens the efforts of the artists clever
And makes the toiler an indolent shirk.
It weakens, the soul of the man with a vision
It greets honest toiling with open derision
And make fun of the hopes and dreams of man.
By perseverance I made it to where I am today.
With a steady persistence in a course of action
In- spite of, difficulties and discouragement,
I gave more traction.

THE PHONE CALL

Mobile and digital networking have speed-up communication.
Calling and messaging to nears and dears,
imparts satisfaction.
Everyone is used to fast telecommunication.
Sometimes unknown phone calls
disturb our assumptions.
Once there was a phone call from a girl,
Who was surrounded by off elements,
She had asked me for refuge at my place;
It was midnight and I was all alone.
I called up to the nearest police station.
Luckily, they picked up the phone
and advised me without any hesitation.
Not to answer the call or the knock at the door.
Within an hour, a phone call and knock on the door.
A girl was shouting for help, thrice
I was scared but had followed police' advice.
Next day, the mystery was solved by the newspaper.
The phone call was tracked by
and thieves were behind bars.

JUNGLE COTTAGE

It was mid-night, we were staying in a jungle cottage (at Jim Corbett)
Early dinner was advised by forest rangers.
It was chilling winter.
We were in our cozy beds, without any further.
Suddenly, there was a loud tiger's roar!
The tourists enjoying bon-fire,
Were now running halter shelter.
We checked our doors and windows.
There were caws of crows.
Our cottage was enveloped by dense fog.
It was sleepless night, till break of dawns.
Next day we were roaming quietly in a closed jungle safari.
Passing through high grassland along a stream.
We saw pug-marks near the stream on soft soil.
Again, got afraid to nearby tigers
And returned- back to our cozy jungle cottage.
It was wonderful experience of jungle cottage,

ROSES AND THORNS

Roses are always surrounded by thorns,
As if the beautiful flowers have protection by thorns.
Roses have sweet smell and full of enormous beauty
Soft, delicate, velvety petals
attract each Tom, Dick and Harry.
If someone likes to pluck the rose
Thorns prick the fingers.
It is nature's play of course.
Love speaks in roses.
Rose is symbol of beauty, soft-ness and balance.
Life is thickly sown with thorns,
But that depends on our glance.
Their smiles of softness with beauty are adorable.
Roses are profusions
Bloom along our lawn.
They are pink, yellow, red and white.
There are thorns too,
Standing guard among the blooms.

WITHERED ROSE

The red rose has withered away
In its own slow motion
On the outcome of the day.
All the red fragrant, delicate petals,
Have withered away.
It has blossomed in a life,shortest .
But its beauty had fulfilled to its fullest
We humans also can live a life to the fullest.
Enriched by our qualities' brightness.
May our life spread the waves of humanity's.
For us, life is a reality.
We have blessings, kindness', memories
And sacrifices to shower.
We live not in years but in deeds.
So of love, peace, harmony and happiness they steeds.

AUTUMN

I love the autumn season.
For me, it is full of life and perfection.
I feel the cool breezes
Slowly falling leaves, put me on ease.
I feel natures miracle
Its relaxing to hear leaves' rustle.
I love woolens
I feel cozy with them.
My elated soul leaves a nice shadow
On my happy face and fine eyebrows'.
I welcome autumn.
With open heart, without any confusion.
With my lovely face and beautiful smile.
I send the message to enjoy every season.
It may be in busy days or any vacations.
Life is short, enjoy it my dear companions.

MIRTH

An odyssey's throughout the hurdles.
Yet a blessing it is to dwell on the earth.
Aiming to destination beloved,
Chasing sweet dreams of mirth.
Through success and failure,
Amid joys and wows
Since birth.
Life can be hurricanes and storm,
But living it, justifies its worth.
Sometimes life beams with hopes
Sometimes disperses in thrones.
Navigating peace and turfs'
Undulating with highs and lows.
Life rejects doldrums and sorrows
Aspiring boldly to sunny and horizons
Hoisting endeavors of morrow.
Life stumbles and falls
Endearing as it learns to walk.

COBALT STARRY NIGHT

Above us stars,
Beneath us constellations.
Five billion of miles away
A galaxy like snowflakes
Falling on ice-cold water.
Far away some farmers
Feeling the chill of that.
Distantly deaths of some stars
Clinching my eyes closed
As I wish with all my might.
I release my visions to the stars above
Watch them shine, watch them spattering
With much passion and love.
Though they are glowing on cobalt blue sky.
Yet they brighten my nights.
Many constellations, such beautiful sights.
Create soft feeling,
Which I love in my life.
The stars glow brighter,
as I enjoy the sights on the blue sky.
Thank you for making all things bright.
I love cobalt blue starry night.

ONSET OF BEAUTIFUL EVENINGS

At the sun set
And passing of beautiful evening
With dull orange lighting.
Somewhere, two individuals are shaking hands.
With some thoughts for tomorrows
There is no questions of sorrows.
As if they are parting,
With joys and deep feelings.
As we say promises are made to be broken,
But sometimes they are made for ever.
They are cherished like sweet memories forever.
They are thought for more and more.
The empty bench,
Is proof of their long talks.
Their love may sublime.
The sun set and on set of evenings,
Keep their secrets.

DAIRY

Since childhood I always pen down,
Many happening, occurring a round.
On my lovely diary.
My diary is my private property.
To pen down my emotions is satisfactory.
Writing is my passion,
Noting down many things on different occasions,
Turning back on bygone- days,
Imparts satisfaction.
A diary keeps one's joys and sorrows.
It reminds our life's turfs and furrows.
Though our brain's computer has lot of storage,
Maintaining a nice diary requires lot of courage.
One must keep his/her diary up-to date.
There is more love, not hate.
A diary keeps many secrets
Many pleasant and unpleasant experiences

THE PRAYERS

The prayer is an act of communication by human with God.
Let us say a prayer for all the people,
who are sick.
Let us say a prayer for all the people,
who are less fortunate.
Let us say a prayer for the people,
who are entangled (among inhuman acts)
Let us say a prayer for the people,
who are mentally sick,
Without any fault, they are pricked.
Let us say a prayer for the people,
who are hard task masters,
But are ill- treated by their own masters.
Let us say a prayer for the people,
who are perished,
Although they are honest
but remain suppressed.
Let us say a prayer for child laborers,
Who under pressure are bound to work.
Let us say a prayer for girl child,
Who do compromises on every step but cries.

WHO AM I SUPPOSED TO BE

I am made to understand who I am?
Since I have a healthy body and sound mind,
Life has taught me, many lessons,
Which are very interesting I find.
Life is associated with positive self- views.
Now I am full of life's varied hues.
Life experiences of failures, made me confident
Now I am resilient.
I am fearless but hate double standards.
First of all I am a nice human- being
I deal with uncertainty, never crying.
I am beautiful creation of God.
Being human and looking forward to, is my nature.
I am doing charity and thinking about my future.

THE ROAD TRIP

Nowadays road trips are popular.
Road trips are safer.
Recently we had a road trip to Wagah borders.
We passed through Ambala, Chandigarh, Pinjore.
Then halted at Amritsar.
We enjoyed the beauty of Punjab.
There we saw moving beautiful moons.
We enjoyed variety of Punjab cousin.
Golden temple, Jalianwala- Bagh, museums have lots of history.
We were touched by people's beauty, honesty and simplicity.
Wagah border is an amazing place.
People on both sides of border were singing patriotic songs.
Salutes and marching of guards of both sides was applauded.
Pleasantries were exchanged.
Then sun was setting up.
Then we were returning- back, to our hotel.
Next day we were driving back to our abode with sweet memories.
It was an amazing experience of our road trip.

THE CAGED BIRD

The caged bird looks up and down.
Remains silent, no sound.
She tries to fly
In vast open sky.
But has, to remain confined.
Seeing outside is only her time pass.
Eating less and turning her water bowl upside down.
She is very lonely.
Flapping her wings occasionally.
The situation is like an innocent man in prison.
But people enjoy her presence,
In their homes and gardens.
The caged bird is restless forever.
Waiting for her relief somewhere,
Her eyes speak of her inner grief.
Her confinement should be brief.

THE BLUSH

Blushes are rainbow of modesty.
Feeling her glee and affection
The little baby blushes.
On seeing lots of children
the lonely child blushes.
On accepting gifts, wrapped up in colorful wrappers'
Children blush with surprise.
Teenagers blush when accepting red roses,
Happy smiling faces.
On her first date, a girl blushes.
There are lots of fears,
But sweet surprises
Make her comfortable.
On seeing the interviewer first time.
A young aspirant, blushes.
Though confident with his preparations.
On the D-day, the young bride blushes
Hiding her fears and aspirations.
The secret of blush, is to accept the flaws.

THE BRIDE

A bride is like a flower, delicate and beautiful.
Apprehensions of bride about her future,
Remain uncertain,
Though knowing each other.
The D-day the bride always remembers
The greatest is in anyone's life,
Sooner or later.
The pleasant start of the day,
Just two persons in love,
And it ends as husband and wife.
It is a brand- new beginning,
the start of a new journey.
With moments to cherish and treasure.
There will be time,
when the bride and her groom will disagree.
These will surely be out weighs by pleasure.
The bride remembers many words of advices.
When the formula for success of marriage were spoken
But the hidden answers vanish.
When the bond of true love lies unbroken
The bride wants to live happily ever after
As lovers and friends.
It is dawn of new life for bride and her groom.
May success finds its way to your hearts.

RANGOLI

Rangoli is auspicious
It depicts the arrival of festival of light.
Oue mood is filled with delight.
The beautiful diyaas are made and decorated at night.
Home- made decorative, are appropriated by one and all.
Ladies and girls are busy.
They are decorating doorways with splash of colors.
Fine designs are carved with different hues.
People appreciate them with different views.
The festival of light is celebrated for five days.
We exchange gifts and sweets with love and grace.
Candles are lit, fire crackers are heard.
We pray to God, Diwali is here.

ENVELOPES, PAPER, PENS, INKPOT

These are the yesteryears' tools of writing.
No comparison with today's fast messaging.
We were fond of the nice stationary.
Fine papers, scented envelops, pens
and writing pads were necessities.
People were writing long letters carefully.
We were waiting for postman anxiously.
There was insistence for good hand-writing.
Which we were never ignoring.
Fountain-pens were filled with waterman-ink.
All the siblings have same color of inks.
Nice writing pads, pens and envelopes
were our precious possessions.
Long letters from elders were read with affection.
Stationary was nice birth-day gift.
Nowadays i-pads and smart phones
are considered nice gifts.
Times have changed and we are accepting it gracefully.
Internet has changed the speed of the world completely.

A LADY IN DEEP THOUGHTS

Life is an unsolved quiz,
Sometimes easy, sometimes full of fizz.
Planned events fail,
Unplanned work out.
Is there any doubt?
How far I co-operate?
With life's turfs and furrows
How cautiously I put my first foot forward,
The outcome I didn't know.
I am brave
I accept life's challenges (who are)
Sometimes O.K.
Sometimes fake.
Systematic planning is my nature.
Adverse circumstances make me helpless creature.
My mental toughness is blessing.
My approach is always for proper things.

PROMISES

Promises are made to be broken
Hearts that are broken
Tears that are wept
Emotions that are soar.

Like angles in flight
Mobiles that would not ring
Darkness of night
For the friends who let down.

Lies that are told
Battered and dithered
Like tarnished gold
Learn to forgive.

Like God above
Unconditionally
That is love.

WAIT

Life is beautiful but everyone has, to wait.
There are young mothers' prayers
for early development of their toddlers.
Schooling is a long process,
but for the best, parents have, to wait.
Young boys and girls are trying harder for their competitive exams,
But for results they have, to wait.
Well qualified, girls and boys trying hard for jobs
But they have, to wait.
The railway enquiry's announcement for scheduled arrival of trains
Is on time, but the passengers have, to wait.
We are paying exuberant consultation fees, in private hospitals,
But the patients have, to wait.
Girls are brought up with values and traditions, did professional courses,
But for suitable groom, their parents have, to wait.
Senior citizens are on death bed,
but insurance- agents' have, to wait.

IF YOU ARE NOT WITH ME

My dear hubby I can face the world bravely if you are with me.
I accept all the challenges of life if you are with me.
I remain focused if you are with me.
I will try my best for cooking tasty food,
If you are with me.
I pray daily for your well- being,
because I know you are with me.
You are mentally sick but I try my best,
because I know you love and care for me.
I never get annoyed by your questions,
because you remained a nice partner for me.
I discipline you on every front
because you understand me every-time.
I co-operate with your rude behavior
because you did the same, while I was suffering.
I talked, walked and swing by you morning and evening,
Because you are always my pillar of strength.
If you are not with me, my future is bleaker.

HAPPY FRIENDS

Life is like a teacup to be filled to
the brim and enjoyed with friends.
Our friends are the people
who change our lives in wonderful ways.
Friends are the guys who understand our feelings closely.
We share our doubts, emotions
and negativity with them confidently.
We accept the difference they made-up
with their precious smiles
sometimes our own world is brighter
by their company.
Their inspiration allows us to see the sun
when we are lost among clouds.
Those friends who love us, simply for being you.
Our friends share our finest moments and sorrows too.

The happiness provided by rue friends gives special lift.
We realize that friendship is,
one of the God's special gifts.
I am grateful to all my friends till date.

DAWN

Every day begins with a new dawn.
Lots of chores, so many decisions we plan.
At the break of dawn, our thoughts are filled with enthusiasms.
Every day starts with a new story,
For which we do our best though sometimes,
it stops without any end.
Again, there is planning for next day's worries.
Birds sing, as if to welcome the new dawn
The golden sunrays fill the atmosphere with elan.
On country side, every- one is busy at the break of dawn.
Farmers are busy with their cows and bullocks
While young maidens are in rows to fill their pitchers.
Laborers and daily wage earners, with their tiffin boxes,
are seen on cycles,
Dawn is the time of the day, when light first appears
On the sky, before the sun rises.

REFLECTIONS

Nature is magical.
There are beautiful, amazing images of chinar trees
and vegetation on the surface of water.
It is mesmerizing beauty on Dal- lake
It incites the artists' creation.
Dal- lake is the biggest lake on the paradise of earth,
With continuous beauty on its banks.

Lots of tourists enjoy Shikara rides.
It brings us closer to nature far and wide.
Before last year I enjoyed that marvelous sight.,
Beauty of mountains, lakes, flowery gardens, tall trees,
Apple orchards is beyond description.
Come to nature, back to nature.

MAGIC OF LOVE

Nobody understands the magic of love.
Love takes one's peace and patience away.
The lovers neither sleep by night nor rest by day.
The mirror keeps looking every person's face.
Who is the wonder-man it seeks to embrace.

Be it the candle, a rose or it may be the legendary Majnu's case.
Beauty has dragged everyone (in love) to market place.
While in love, all joys in their heart flies
Without failures, nobody cries.

It is only the beginning of love,
And you begin to cry,
you know not the hazards,
that on this path lie.

DEW DROPS

In a village of dreams, we used to live
Fetching water in a sieve.
Look beyond the closed panes, beyond the alcoves
On the green trees, the lush branches, the flowers
How silently the dew drops rain ceaselessly.
Dew drops wet on flowers
After fresh and pretty rain showers.
Dew on petals of different flowers
Beauty so rare.

Dew drops carries in its eyes
Mountains and forests, sea and sky.
With every change of weathers
Contrariwise, a diamond splits,
The prospects into idle bits
That none can put together.

HAND IN HAND

Our toddler are precious gifts of nature.
A toddler is in secure hands,
when he is hand in hand with his father figure.
Feeling of security and love is through touch
Father's cares and affection is so much.
That impart him great satisfaction.
Hand in hand with each other show their bonding and affection.
Senior citizens too feel elated
When their hands are held for support by their children.
Sometimes,
Grand- children follow suit,
to their grand- parents.
Life goes on happily with each other
With love, care and co- operation.

ALL THE WORLD IS A STAGE

This world is a stage and we are the actors of this stage.
All day and night a funny something,
is happening around.
Under the dust raised by me,
I see a desert hidden around.
And the river before me,
rubs its head, on the ground
The temple is in front and the cathedral behind.
My hands are lifeless though,
my eyes are still bright.
Still the world is a stage,
which is full of life, I find.
The loveliness of flowers,
invites us all to enjoy the sight
The eyes should always remain open and bright.
East, west, north, south
there are mirrors above and below.
The world is no longer is a stage,
The difference between right and wrong, you know.

TRIBUTE TO MY FATHER

Did we remember dear dad to thank you enough
For all you have done to us?
For all the times you were by our side
To help and support us to celebrate our successes.
To understand our problems, to accept our defeats.
The value of hard work, judgements, courage and integrity?
We wonder if we ever thanked you, for the sacrifices you made.
To let us have the best?
Simple things—laughter, smiles and times we shared.
We are thankful to from bottom of our heart.
Hoping that you know all along
How much you meant to us.
Thank you for being our angel for life
And making growing up fun.
Let me thinking how truly blessed I am
To have a father as honest, truthful and wonderful.

A HAPPY OLD COUPLE

Love has no age, no limitations and no death.
As we grow older together,
as we continue to change with age,
There is one thing that never will change
I will keep falling in love with you.
Grow old with me together forever, love forever
And sometimes I just look at you
And wonder how many dreams come true.
There is no knowing what tomorrow brings
Or what the autumn, winter, summer, springs
We only know our yester years' glow
And memories of long ago.
The evening dwell on our years.
And summer songs ring for our ears
It takes the toll on, our frames.
We have seen them come and go,
The many shades of life we know.

THE PAST

Today's present will be the past for tomorrow.
Future planning elates us, no for sorrows.
Our past leaves behind footprints of time.
We forget so many negative things behind.
Though past shadows our present
We got alert on our past folies
But our present is somewhat shaky.
The proverb as you sow, so shall you reap.
Alerts us of our past deeds.
Sometimes our past leaves behind sweet memories'.
The revival of those moments, are pleasant stories.
Our past has sweet childhood, teenage
and school days' chats and mischiefs.
Now we smile, why we were so naughty.
Past happenings and activities keep us engaged in our spare time.
It is nice to have a look on our past-time.

THORNS IN THE PATH

Rafiqon se raqeeb achchy jo jal ker bhi naam lety hain.
Gulon se khaar behtar hain jo barh ker daman tham lety hain.
Our life is full of sweet- sour experiences,
sometimes flowering touches.
Sometimes thorny pathways.
Leaving behind footprints of good and grey times.
The touch of thorns of the path are a way, deep telling
Of the senses deep telling,
Of the senses not to bloom.
With out a wish to, without belief in pain to hold as true.
One thorn of experience is
Worth a whole wilderness of warnings.
Why are we messing up thorny paths?
Our stressed situations, are like thorns in our path.
Healing takes its toll.
Our life is like a thorny rose
Not perfect but always beautiful.

SYMPATHY

No to sympathy, yes to moving on.
I have, to face the inevitable.
Please, do not stand at my grave and weep.
I am not there I do not sleep.
Body without soul, is to be forgotten.
I am thousand winds that blow.
I am diamond glint on the snow.
I am the sunlight on the ripen grain.
I am slow gentle autumn rain.
When you wake up in the morning hush
I am the swift uplifting rush
Of the quite birds in circling flight.
I am soft starlight at night.
Sympathy acts to remove the ceaseless sufferings
Of the world in grey times.

SOLITARY JOURNEY

Our life is a solitary journey.
It may be compared with a train journey.
We have many relatives and friends.
Sooner or later, everyone, gets down on his\her destination.
We are surrounded by different persons in various stages of life.
How strange is our last journey,
Without soul body is life less.
Our achievements and assets are all useless.
We arrive in the world, with our fists closed
But we leave the world, with our open hands.
It is the mystery of life really
That our last journey is solitary.
Loneliness is the poverty of self,
Solitude is the richness of self.

DREAM HOME

The home I live now is my dream home,
Where two seniors, a young couple
and two lovely, grand- daughters live.
Everyone is busy from dawn till dusk.
Our breakfast is different for everyone,
But all have same lunch and dinner, which is wholesome.
By God's grace our family is hale and hearty
Our dream home is sweet home because of its unity.
Friends, relatives and guests are always welcome.
Love and help for maids and neighbors are always unconditional.
The foundation of our dream home is on love and affection.
Our principle for happiness, is everyone's satisfaction.
Our young couple spends ample time for their daughters' education.
Our dream home is united on challenging times.
As we all suffered from corona,
But by God's blessings we came back to our dream home fit and fine.

DOCTORS

Doctors use their expertise to heal the patients,
During our illness, doctors prove their worth.
Due to environmental pollution and unhealthy food habits,
sound health is arduous.
Permanent health checkups are crucial.
More worries and mental stress pushing us towards ill health
People worry more about their future,
than realizing that health is wealth.
A doctor gives his patients joy and pleasure
Treat them with multiple complexions.
Doctors' profession is noblest still.
We are happy when you cure the ill.
Observation, reason, human touch
and courage, together make a doctor.
We respect and trust our doctors.
To the best of their ability doctors serve the humanity.

MONSOON DREAMS

70% of our population lives in villages & their main occupation is agriculture.
The monsoon dreams are fine for farmers.
With ample monsoon their crops flourish.
Their hopes and needs, in return, they cherish
.

Dreams are our realities in waiting.
The monsoon clouds laden with flowing, floating rainstorms.
It is continuing for some days.
There is water logging in roads and lanes.
Too much mud clogs the drains.
(Is it crushing monsoon dreams ?)
The surface of earth is covered with vegetation,
Enjoy swings, eat mangoes in tripling rain.
Now we are sitting near window panes, enjoying monsoon dreams.
Life is not about waiting for the storm to pass,
It is about learning to dance in rain.

GAUTAM BUDH TEACHING

The most important lessons, I learnt so far----

Don't let anyone make you cruel.

No matter how badly you want to give them, a taste of their own bitter medicines'.

The mind is everything, what you think you become.

Generosity brings happiness, at every stage of its expression.

We experience joy in forming the intention to be generous.

If you find no one to support you on spiritual path, walk alone.

All that we are is the result of what we have thought.

May all beings have happy minds.

Guard your mind against negative thoughts.

What you think you become?

Work out your own salvation.

If you truly love yourself, you could never hurt others.

Everything changes, nothing remains without change.

MONSOON CELEBRATIONS

Someone is soaking in rain again and again.
Natural cool rain soothes mind and body.
How beautiful is the rain
It is pleasant sight, human love of rain.
Now it is as if a dream come true.
Nowadays people, are scared- of soaking in rain water
As if they will catch up cold and fever.
Though rain water contains many
useful elements and dissolved nitrogen.
Sometimes heavy rains result in clocked drains
Overflowing of water bodies and muddy roads.
It is hazardous to touch any electric poles.
Soaked electric wires and cables are dangerous.
In our childhood we enjoyed rain on our roof tops.
No fever or sour throats.
Completely drenched but ate lots of mangoes and roasted corn-cobs.
Rain was boon for our health and complexions.